P9-CAM-776

RANDY'S CORNER

DAY BY DAY WITH...

GABBY DOUGLAS

BY
JOANNE MATTERN

Mitchell Lane
PUBLISHERS
P.O. Box 196
Hockessin, Delaware 19707
Visit us on the web: www.mitchelllane.com
Comments? Email us:
mitchelllane@mitchelllane.com

Mitchell Lane
PUBLISHERS

Printing   2   3   4   5   6   7   8   9

RANDY'S CORNER

DAY BY DAY WITH...

Alex Morgan	Manny Machado
Beyoncé	Mia Hamm
Bindi Sue Irwin	Miley Cyrus
Chloë Moretz	Missy Franklin
Dwayne "The Rock" Johnson	Selena Gomez
Eli Manning	Shaun White
Gabby Douglas	Stephen Hillenburg
Justin Bieber	Taylor Swift
LeBron James	Willow Smith

Library of Congress Cataloging-in-Publication Data
Mattern, Joanne, 1963–
Day by day with Gabby Douglas / by Joanne Mattern.
   pages cm. — (Randy's corner)
Includes bibliographical references and index.
ISBN 978-1-61228-451-4 (library bound)
1. Douglas, Gabrielle, 1995– —Juvenile literature. 2. Women gymnasts—United States—Biography—Juvenile literature. 3. Women Olympic athletes—United States—Biography—Juvenile literature. I. Title.
GV460.2.D88M37 2014
796.44092—dc23
                                                      2013023043

eBook ISBN: 9781612285108

ABOUT THE AUTHOR: Joanne Mattern is the author of many nonfiction books. She especially enjoys writing biographies of famous people. Joanne has watched the Olympic Games every year they have been held since 1968. She enjoys learning about the dedicated athletes who take part in the Games. She lives in New York State with her husband, four children, and several pets.

PUBLISHER'S NOTE: The following story has been thoroughly researched and to the best of our knowledge represents a true story. While every possible effort has been made to ensure accuracy, the publisher will not assume liability for damages caused by inaccuracies in the data and makes no warranty on the accuracy of the information contained herein. This story has not been authorized or endorsed by Gabby Douglas.

The young lady ran across the mat. She jumped and flipped. She spun and danced. The crowd cheered and clapped.

Who is this girl who can twist and turn with amazing grace? It is Gabby Douglas!

MOTHER NATALIE

SISTER JOY

Gabrielle Christina Victoria Douglas was born on December 31, 1995, in Newport News, Virginia. She was the youngest child and has two older sisters and one older brother. Gabby's mom, Natalie Hawkins, raised the family by herself.

Gabby's sister Arielle taught her how to do cartwheels when Gabby was four years old. Soon Gabby was teaching herself new tricks.

GABBY IS BEING HUGGED BY HER AUNT, BIANCA WILLIAMS, AFTER SHE ARRIVES FOR A VISIT TO HER HOME IN VIRGINIA BEACH. GABBY'S SISTER ARIELLE HAWKINS IS FAR LEFT. HER BROTHER, JOHN DOUGLAS, IS SHOWN IN THE CENTER.

GABBY PRACTICES HER MOVES
ON THE BALANCE BEAM WITH
EASE AND GRACE.

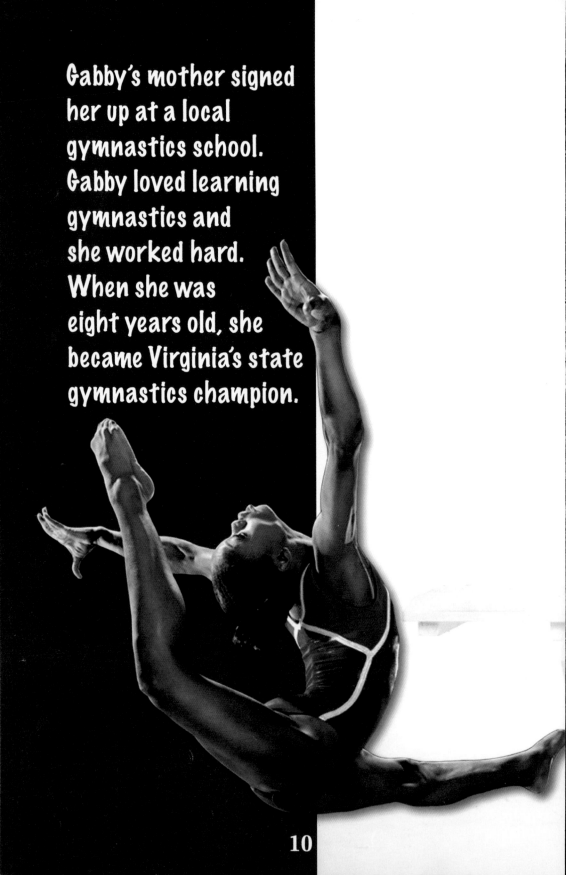

Gabby's mother signed
her up at a local
gymnastics school.
Gabby loved learning
gymnastics and
she worked hard.
When she was
eight years old, she
became Virginia's state
gymnastics champion.

Gabby wanted to be in the Olympics. She wanted to work with a famous coach named Liang Chow. But Coach Chow lived in Iowa, far away from Gabby's home in Virginia. She asked her mom to let her move to Iowa. Gabby's family did not want her to go. But if Gabby was going to be in the Olympics, she needed to train with the best. Finally, they said yes.

Gabby moved to Iowa in 2010. She lived with Travis and Missy Parton and their children. Gabby missed her family, but she liked living with the Partons. And she loved training with Coach Chow!

MISSY
PARTON

16

Gabby trained for hours every day. She spent lots of time taking classes and studying, too. She missed her family a lot. It was a hard life, but Gabby loved it.

Soon Gabby was going to big competitions. In 2011, she won third place on the uneven bars in the Visa Championships. Then she went to Japan for the World Championships with the American team. Gabby did a good job. Her team won first place in the team all-around event. Her fans began calling her the Flying Squirrel!

In 2012, Gabby tried out for the Olympics and she made the US team! The Olympics are the biggest sporting event in the world. Now Gabby had to train harder than ever.

In July, Gabby and her teammates went to London to compete in the Olympic Summer Games. Everyone called the team "The Fierce Five." Gabby and the United States team did great! Gabby won a gold medal. The American team won a gold medal too. For Gabby, it was a dream come true!

FROM LEFT, JORDYN WIEBER, GABRIELLE DOUGLAS, MCKAYLA MARONEY, ALEXANDRA RAISMAN, AND KYLA ROSS

Suddenly Gabby was famous. She was on television shows. She met First Lady Michelle Obama.

FIRST LADY MICHELLE OBAMA AND GABBY DOUGLAS APPEAR ON *THE TONIGHT SHOW WITH JAY LENO*. LENO HOLDS GABBY'S OLYMPIC GOLD MEDAL.

Gabby and her teammates appeared in the Macy's Thanksgiving Day Parade.

FROM LEFT, ALEXANDRA RAISMAN, GABBY DOUGLAS, AND MCKAYLA MARONEY RIDE A FLOAT IN THE MACY'S THANKSGIVING DAY PARADE IN NEW YORK. BEING PART OF THE PARADE WAS A LOT OF FUN FOR GABBY AND HER TEAMMATES. IT WAS A GREAT HONOR AS WELL.

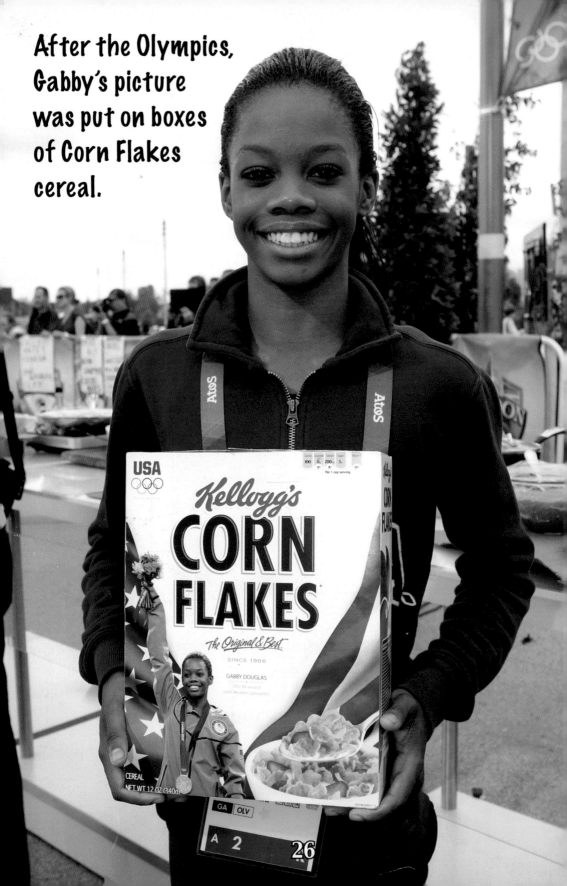

After the Olympics, Gabby's picture was put on boxes of Corn Flakes cereal.

Gabby is excited to be a hero and a role model. She says that anyone can make their dreams come true with hard work!

GABBY'S MOM

Gabby knows it's important to help other people, too. In 2012, she helped people fighting cancer by appearing in the Stand Up to Cancer telethon. This event raised money to help find a cure for the disease.

Gabby loves having fun with her teammates. She also loves spending time with her family. But Gabby has a lot of work to do. She still trains several hours a day. She wants to compete in the Olympics again in 2016.

London 2012

Lond

GABBY TOOK HOME THE YOUNGSTARS AWARD AT THE 2013 BET AWARDS

Gabby Douglas is a great athlete. She is also a great person. Gabby knows that hard work will pay off. Her hard work made her one of the best gymnasts. Her hard work made her a star!

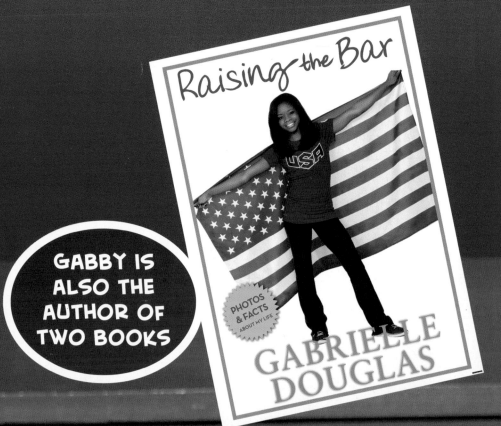

Raising the Bar

PHOTOS
& FACTS
ABOUT MY LIFE

GABRIELLE
DOUGLAS

GABBY IS ALSO THE AUTHOR OF TWO BOOKS

FURTHER READING

BOOKS

Fishman, Jon M. *Gabby Douglas*. Minneapolis: Lerner Publishing Group, 2013.

Mara, Wil. *Gymnastics*. New York: Children's Press, 2012.

Simkins, Kate. *I Want to Be a Gymnast*. New York: DK Readers, 2006.

Tieck, Sarah. *Gabby Douglas: Historic Olympic Champion*. Edina, Minnesota: Big Buddy Books, 2013.

ON THE INTERNET

NBCNews.com: "Lester Holt Interviews Gold Medalist Gabby Douglas" http://www.nbcnews.com/video/dateline/48713122

Sports Illustrated Kids: "Classic Photos of Gabby Douglas" http://www.sikids.com/photos/44656/classic-photos-of-gabby-douglas/1

USA Gymnastics http://www.usagym.org

WORKS CONSULTED

ABC News. "Barbara Walters' 10 Most Fascinating People: Gabby Douglas." December 12, 2012. http://abcnews.go.com/Entertainment/video/barbara-walters-10-fascinating-people-gabby-douglas-17952263

Associated Press. "Tom Hanks, Gabrielle Douglas, Other Stars Join 'Stand Up To Cancer' Telethon." September 5, 2012.

Biography.com. "Gabby Douglas." http://www.biography.com/people/gabby-douglas-20900057

Douglas, Gabrielle, and Michelle Burford. *Grace, Gold, and Glory: My Leap of Faith*. Grand Rapids, MI: Zondervan, 2012.

The Official Website of Gabrielle Douglas. http://gabrielledouglas.com

Park, Alice. "Gabby Douglas: Team USA's Flip Artist." Time, July 19, 2012.

INDEX

PHOTO CREDITS: Cover—Nick Laham/Getty Images; pp. 4–5—Miguel Medina/AFP/Getty Images; pp. 3, 19, 28—Streeter Lecka/Getty Images; p. 4—Ezra Shaw/Getty Images; pp. 6–7, 8—AP Photo/Virginian-Pilot, Ross Taylor; pp. 8–9, 13—AP Photo/Jeff Roberson; pp. 10, 11, 23—cc-by-sa; p. 12—AP Photo/Jae C. Hong; pp. 14–15—AP Photo/Charles Rex Arbogast; p. 15—David Eulitt/Kansas City Star/MCT via Getty Images; pp. 16–17, pp. 18–19—Ronald Martinez/Getty Images; p. 17—AP Photo/Charlie Krupa; p. 20, 22—AP Photo/Gregory Bull; p. 21—Thomas Coex/AFP/Getty Images; p. 24—AP Photo/NBC, Margaret Norton; p. 25—AP Photo/Charles Sykes; p. 26—Scott Halleran/Getty Images for Kelloggs; p. 27—Gregg DeGuire/WireImage/Getty Images; p. 29—Mike Windle/Getty Images for BET; pp. 30–31—Andy Kropa/Getty Imags. Every effort has been made to locate all copyright holders of materials used in this book. Any errors or omissions will be corrected in future editions of the book.